Notes On The History And Text Of Our Early English Bible: And Of Its Translation Into Welsh...

George Leader Owen

NOTES

ON THE

HISTORY AND TEXT

OF

Our Early English Bible,

AND OF ITS

Translation into Welsh.

BY

GEORGE LEADER OWEN,

OF

WITHYBUSH, IN THE COUNTY OF PEMBROKE,

SOMETIME SCHOLAR OF TRINITY HALL,

AND

BACHELOR OF LAWS IN THE UNIVERSITY OF CAMBRIDGE.

London :

SIMPKIN, MARSHALL, HAMILTON, KENT AND CO., LTD.

Cheltenham :

F. GASTRELL AND SON, MONTPELLIER EXCHANGE.

1901.

Divinity School.

Whilst these pages have been passing through the press, the dark shadow of night has fallen on the land, and the greatest figure of the world has passed away. One whose name was, is, and ever will be, one of the best-loved memories of the Empire ruled so long by the Great White Queen,

VICTORIA:

A Queen whose absolutely loyal adhesion to the lines of her sovereign constitutional rule, provoked from her people, on their part, an unprecedented offering of devoted loyalty;

A Monarch, under whose beneficent sway the kingdom she came to rule, so long ago, expanded into an Empire, on which the sun never sets, the greatest the world has seen;

But above and beyond these a Woman whose purity of life—as wife and mother —whose loving sympathy with the poorest of her subjects in their sorrow, whose majestic carriage of her own deep griefs, drew from the whole civilized world, when, alas! we lost her,

A TRIBUTE OF TEARS.

SOME NOTES ON THE TEXT

OF OUR

Early English Bible.

" To my early knowledge of the Bible I owe the best part of my taste in literature, and the most precious and, on the whole, the one essential part of my education."—RUSKIN.

" Amongst all our national treasures the greatest is the English Bible. Unique amongst books in its unapproachable dignity and grandeur, it holds amongst us an undisputed pre-eminence as the most splendid literary monument that we possess of the genius of our native tongue."—H. W. HOARE.

To the student of English words no books are so rich, both in interest and instruction, as the older versions of our Bible, although down to the time of Wycliffe the translations were only fragmentary. But in them may be read the history of the language of England from the Anglo-Saxon days of Alfred the Great down to the reign of Queen Victoria.

Before referring to those versions, a brief outline of the sources from which our English translations are derived may be of interest.

It is a curious fact that although the Books of the Old Testament were originally written in Hebrew, the two oldest copies known to the world are translations into Greek and Latin.

The oldest *Hebrew* manuscript in existence is of little earlier date than William the Conqueror. All the old Hebrew MSS. before A.D. 900 have vanished from the earth.

In the Preface to The Revised Version of 1885 it is stated that the earliest Hebrew MS. of the Scriptures, of which the age is certainly known, bears date A.D. 916.

The oldest version of the Old Testament known in the present day, and among the first collections of the Holy Writings ever made, is the Greek translation called :

THE SEPTUAGINT, OR THE BIBLE OF THE SEVENTY.

It was so called because the number of translators was supposed to have been about seventy.

It was translated about 280 B.C. by command of Ptolemy Philadelphus from very ancient Hebrew MSS., by Jewish Scholars of Alexandria, and is supposed to have perished, with many thousands of other MSS., when the Library of Alexandria was destroyed by fire during the siege of the City by Julius Cæsar. Three copies, however, in the Greek tongue, are still extant, and one of the three is, curiously enough, in the hands of each of the great divisions of the Christian Church :

I.—THE ALEXANDRINE MANUSCRIPT (Codex A), presented to Charles 1st. A.D. 1628, by the then Patriarch of Constantinople, is in the possession of the Protestant Church in the British Museum.

II.—THE VATICAN MANUSCRIPT has been in the custody of the Roman Catholics for some five centuries, and is kept in the Library of the Papal Palace at Rome.

III.—And the SINAITIC MANUSCRIPT, discovered by Professor Tischendorf in 1844 at the Convent of St. Catherine at the foot of the mountain, is guarded by the priests of the Greek Church at St. Petersburg. The Codex Sinaiticus is, of the three Codices, the most ancient.

But although these MSS. are the oldest known copies of the Bible in the world, being supposed to date from between 300 and 450 A.D., they were not discovered till comparatively recent times, and neither of them was known to the translators of the Authorised Version of 1611. The first time they were used by English translators was in the preparation of the Revised Version of 1885, of which more hereafter.

The Septuagint contained those Sacred Writings that we now know as "The Old Testament," a name first given to them (as far as we know) by the Apostle Paul (2 Cor. iii, 14) : "For until this day remaineth the same vail untaken away in the reading of the Old Testament." It also contained those books which we now call "The Apocrypha"—or "things hidden"—which in the Great Bible and others of that date were called Hagiographa, or sacred writings.

The term "New Testament" occurs first. (St. Mark, xiv, 24) "This is my blood of the New Testament." The name "Bible" is supposed to have been given to the whole collection of these writings by S. Chrysostom in the 5th. century.

It is a somewhat curious fact, and worthy of note, that the last verses (9-20) of the last chapter of St. Mark's Gospel, in which Christ is alleged to have given to His disciples the miraculous powers afterwards claimed by the Priests of Holy Church, are not to be found in the two older of the three MSS., viz.: the Vatican and the Sinaitic.

The next great Version of the Bible given to the world, about three centuries after Christ, contained the Old and the New Testaments, and was in the Latin tongue. It is commonly known as

The Latin Vulgate of St. Jerome.

It was prepared by the great scholar Eusebius Hieronymus about A.D. 385, the Old Testament being translated directly from the Hebrew.

The Vulgate is said to have been translated into Latin, for the use of the Latin speaking Church in North Africa, during the fourth Century. S. Jerome by his great knowledge of languages and his wonderful energy, did more than any man who ever lived towards the interpretation of the Holy Scriptures. He was born in Dalmatia about A.D. 329, and acquired his knowledge of Hebrew in the Syrian deserts, and thus was able to translate the Bible from Hebrew into Latin.

The Vulgate was for nearly a thousand years the parent of every version of the Scriptures in Western Europe. It was the only Bible from which the early Anglo-Saxon fragmentary translations were made—as the knowledge of Greek and Hebrew was then practically non-existent—and it has left its imprint on our own Authorised Version.

It was from this version that John Wycliffe and his fellow-labourers, about a thousand years later, translated the first English Bible. From this version also, the Roman

Catholic Rhemish and Douay versions are taken, and in the words of Mr. Paterson Smyth:—"It was the parent of every version of the Scriptures in Western Europe for more than ten centuries." In fact, it was the origin of all our translations of the Bible till the time of William Tyndale.

From the time of St. Jerome the Bible remained for many centuries entombed in Latin, "a tongue not understanded of the people." It was available only to "the Clerks" and other erudite persons, and was a sealed book to the mass of the Laity—the lewd people. How it got eventually into their language and into their hands, is it not written in the Book of the Martyrs?

The Versions of the English Bible in Chronological Order.

———•◦•———

I.—Translations from the Latin Vulgate A.D. 385.

> 7th. to 14th. Centuries:—Fragments of the Psalms, Gospels, &c., made by Alfred the Great and by Anglo-Saxon Monks and others, before the invention of Printing.

> A.D. 1382. The Manuscript Version of Wycliffe and Nicholas de Hereford.

> 1388. Revision of the same by John Purvey, also MS.

———————

II.—Printed Translations from the Hebrew, Greek and other languages.

> 1525. Tyndale's New Testament ⎫ From the original
> 1530. Tyndale's Old Testament ⎬ Hebrew and Greek

> 1535. Coverdale's Bible, translated "out of Latin and Dutch," as stated by himself.

> 1537. Mathew's Bible ⎫ Practically a Revision of
> 1539. Taverner's Bible ⎬ Coverdale's Bible.

> 1539. The first Edition of the Great Bible.

> 1560. The Genevan Bible.

> 1568. The Bishops' Bible.

> 1611. THE AUTHORISED VERSION.

III.—A Translation from the same sources, with the addition of the Alexandrian, the Vatican, and the Sinaitic Codices.

The Revised Version of 1885.

In the Anglo-Saxon times some fragments of the Bible were translated into English, but it must be borne in mind that the Anglo-Saxon of that age is no more the English of to-day, than the Latin Vulgate is modern Italian. Amongst them the best known are:

The Gospel of St. John by the Venerable Bede, about A.D. 700; (the first portion of the New Testament translated into the vernacular language of this country); the Ten Commandments and some fragments of Exodus by King Alfred the Great were also translated sometime in the 9th. century.

Of the best known author of these early fragments— often rather adaptations than translations—a recent writer says—"During the 7th. century, in the beautiful Abbey of St. Hilda, that hangs over the waves of the North Sea on the cliffs of the White Town of the North, Cœdmon, a Whitby monk (we are told by the Venerable Bede, the grand old monk of Jarrow), had sung the story of the Creation of the world, and of man, and had left verses on other histories of Holy Writ."

Bede himself, who, says Mr. Dore, "was one of the brightest gems in the Crown of the Church of England," left as a precious legacy to the Church he loved, a translation of the Gospel of S. John.

About the close of the 7th. century the Psalter was translated into Anglo-Saxon by Guthlac, a Saxon anchorite, and another version of the Psalter was made shortly afterwards by S. Aldhem, Abbot of Malmsbury, afterwards Bishop of Sherburne.

Ælfric, another monk, in the 10th. century, translated the first seven books of the Old Testament: however, all these were but fragmentary, they were paraphrases rather than translations, and it was not until the 14th. century that the real work of translation was commenced.

King Alfred's translation of the Ten Commandments is a most interesting specimen of the language spoken in England at that day ; it commences thus:

Drihten was sprecende thæs worde to Moyse, and thus cwœth :—
Ic am Drihten thy God. Ic the sit gelœdde of
Aegypta londe and of heora threow dome.
No lufa-thu othre fremde godas ofer me.

.   .   .   .

Which is, translated literally into modern English :

The Lord was speaking these words to Moses and thus said (quoth) :
I am the Lord thy God. I led thee out of Egypt's land and its thraldom.
Love not other strange Gods over me.

.   .   .   .

It is curious that the word Drihten, the Anglo-Saxon word commonly used to ascribe to God or Christ the title of Lord, should have completely disappeared from our language. It is found in use as late as A.D. 1320 in a metrical paraphrase of the Bible called 'Cursor Mundi' by an unknown author:

"Thoru the might of Sant Drihten:"
(Through the might of the Holy Lord.)
Visit of the Magi.

.   In Wycliffe's Bible the above verses run thus :—

" And the lord spak alle these wordis :
I am the lord God that ladde the out of the lond of egypt fro the house of *servage.*
thou schalt not have alien goddis before me."

In a MS. belonging to Bishop Bonner, for which he claimed in A.D. 1555 an age of eight score years, the words are :—

"And the Lord speek alle these wordes.
I am the lord thi god that hath lad the out of the londe of Egypte from the house of *thraldom.*
thou shalt not have alyen goddis before me."

And in Bishop Coverdale's Bible A.D. 1535 it is thus rendered :—

"And the Lorde spake all these wordes and sayde.

I am the Lorde thy God which have brought the out of the londe of Egipte from the house of *bondage.*

Thou shalt have none other goddis in my sight."

In our Bible of 1611 (Exodus xx, 1) it reads:

"And God spake all these words saying

I am the Lord thy God which have brought thee out of the land of Egypt, out of the house of bondage.

Thou shalt have no other gods before me.

A metrical version of the Old and New Testaments called "Sowlehele" was published in the 14th. century, as also a metrical version of the Psalms: and a Prose Psalter by Richard Rolle de Hampole, author of the "Prick of Conscience," an Augustine Monk, A.D. 1340; and several other fragmentary translations. Of his own translation of the Psalter, Richard Rolle, the Yorkshire monk, better known as the hermit of Hampole, quaintly says:—

" In this work I seke no straunge Ynglys, bot lightest and communest, and swilk that is most like unto the Latyne, so y^t. thai that knowes noght ye Latyne, be (by) the Ynglys, may come to manie Latyne words.

In the Translacion I felogh (follow) the letter als-mekill (as much) as I may, and tho I find no proper Ynglys I felogh the wit of the words, so that thai that shall read it shall not drede erring. In the expowning I felogh holie Doctors. For it may comen into sum envious mannes honde, that knowis not what he sul saye, that will saye that I wist not, what I sayed, and so do harm tille (to) hym and tylle other."

The Saxon words of these early translators are often more terse, strong, and simple than our modern equivalents, and it is almost a matter of regret that we have not retained some of the expressive words of Archbishop Ælfric, who speaks of a centurion as a 'hundred man'; of a disciple as a 'learning cnight' (youth). The man with the dropsy he calls 'the water-sick man'; the treasury is 'the gold-hoard'; and Sunday is 'the reste daeg' (the rest day.)

It will interest the student of Anglo-Saxon and English to compare the language of the successive translations of the Bible, and an instance is given below of the 15th. Psalm, the first text being taken from the Northumbrian Metrical Psalter (A.D. 1260), the second from Nicholas Hereford's Version of the Psalms, A.D. 1380, and the third from our Authorised Version.

Metrical Psalter, A.D. 1260.

1.—Lavard. in thi telde who sal wone?
    In thi hali hille or wha reste mone?

2.—Whilke that incomes wemles,
    And ai wirkes rightwisenes.

3.—That spekes sotbnes in hert his,
    And noght did swikeldom in tung his,
    Ne did to his neghburgh ivel ne gram,
    Ne ogaines his neghburgh upbraiding nam.

. . . . . .

5.—Ne his silver til okir noght es givand
    Ne giftes took over, underhand;
    That does these night and dai,
    Not sal he be stired in ai. (aye).

II.

Hereford's Psalter, A.D. 1380.

1.—Lord who shal duelle in thi tabernacle
    or who shall eft resten in thi holy hil?

2.—That goth in without wem, and
    werkith ryztt wisness.

3.—That speketh treuth in his herte
    that did not trecherie in his tunge,
    Ne did to his neyhbore evel.
    And reprof toc not agen his neyboris.

. . . . . .

5.—That his monce yaf not to usure
and gifts upon the innocent toc not
He that doth these thingns,
Shall not be moved into without ende.

III.

Authorised Version, A.D. 1611.

1.—Lord, who shall abide in Thy tabernacle ?
Who shall dwell in thy holy hill ?

2.—He that walketh uprightly, and worketh
righteousness
and speaketh the truth in his heart.

3.—He that backbiteth not with his tongue,
nor doeth evil to his neighbour,
nor taketh up a reproach against his neighbour.

.   .   .   .   .   .

5.—He that putteth not out his money to usury,
nor taketh reward against the innocent.
He that doeth these things shall never be
moved.

In the 15th. Psalm from the Metrical Psalter are several words that have either become obsolete, or have so changed their features as to be no longer recognizable :—

LAVARD : is an old spelling of our word *Lord,* when it was in a transition state between 'Hlaford' (as it was spelt by earlier writers) and our modern word 'Lord.' It was applied in the 13th. century, as it is to-day, to the Deity, as well as to a nobleman. The word 'Hlaford' or 'Hlafweard' was originally derived from two Anglo-Saxon words Hlaf = a loaf, and Weard = a warden, and the 'Lord' originally was only the *Loaf-keeper.* In the same way the old word Hlafdigè, or *Lady,* meant the Loaf-kneader. These are instances of words that, as Archbishop Trench says, "have risen in life." But the following illustration of the rise in life of words is perhaps even more remarkable. By a gradual development—the humble offices of *Sty-ward* [Sty: an inclosure for swine.—PROF. SKEAT] and that of an equally humble one, the *Hogward* or keeper of the hogs—

have given the name of Stewart to a Royal house and of Howard to a ducal one.

TELDE :—a tent or tabernacle, remaining with us in the form of "tilt" a booth or canvas covering.

MONE :—may or shall. The Freemasons still use this verb in their ritual in the sense of Amen. They say—"So *mote* it be."

WEMLESS :—spotless, is used by Wycliffe in his Psalter.

SOTHNESS :—truth—"In good sooth," although it has fallen out of modern parlance, appears frequently in the works of Shakespeare and more recent authors.

SWIKELDOM :—treachery, alsoused in Layamon's "Brut" A.D. 1205, is quite obsolete, and the same may be said of GRAM = anger.

NAM:—to take, survives only in the first syllable of '*nimble*,' of which word the original sense is "to take as one's share"—(SKEAT), but is perpetuated in the name of one of Falstaff's followers—Corporal *Nym*, who acquired this cognomen from his habit of 'taking'—*generally* what did not belong to him.

The following specimen of Hampole's Psalter—the first translation into English prose—is interesting as shewing how, as early as the year A.D. 1340, the Anglo-Saxon language was hardening, or perhaps we should say softening, down into the English we now speak.

The specimen chosen is the 23rd. Psalm—"The Lord is my Shepherd, &c.," which is too well known to require to be placed here for comparison.

Our lord governeth me : and nothing to me shal wante : stede of pasture that he me sette.

In the water of hetyng forth he me broughte : my soule he turnyde.

He ladde me on in the stretis of rygtwisnesse: for his name.

For win gif I hadde goo in the myddil of the shadewe of deeth: I shall not dreede yveles: for thou art with me.

Thi geerde and thi staf: thei have comfirted me. Thou hast greythid in my sygt a bord agens them that angryn me:

Thou fattide myn heved in oyle: and my chalys drunkenyng what is cleer.

And thi mercy shall folewe me: in alle the dayes of my lyf.

And that I wone in the hous of oure lord in the lengthe of days.

But no general translation of the Scriptures was attempted until the time of one of the most striking and sterling characters of our history, the pure and patriotic Parish Priest of Lutterworth—JOHN WYCLIFFE, sometime Master of Balliol College, Oxford.

A very interesting and strong version of the Psalms is that written in the Broad Scotch Dialect by Dr. P. H. Waddell, one of which runs thus:—

PSALM XXIII. (A. V.)

The sheep-keeping of the Lord's kind and canny, wi' a braw howff at lang last: David keeps his sheep, the Lord keeps David.

1.—The Lord is my herd, nae want sal fa' me.

2.—He lowts me till lie among green howes: He airts me atowre by the lown watirs;

3.—He wakens my wa-gaen saul; He weises me roun, for His ain Names Sake, intil right roddins.

4.—Na! tho' I gang thro' the dead-mirk-dail; e'en there sal I dread nae skaithen: for Yersel are nar-by me. Yer stok and Yer stay haud me baith fu' cheerie.

5.—My buird Ye hae hanselled in face o' my faes; Ye hae drookit my head wi' oyle; my bicker is fu' an' skailin.

6.—E'en sae, sai gude-guidin and gude-gree gang wi' me, ilk day o' my living; and ever mair syne, i' the Lord's ain howff at lang last, sal I mak byden.

This edition of the Psalms was quaintly entitled:—

"The Psalms, frae Hebrew intil Scottis."

The headings of many of the Psalms are pathetically quaint. For instance, the nineteenth Psalm, which begins

(A.V.) "The Heavens declare the Glory of God and the Firmament sheweth His Handiwork" is headed :—

> " God's Lift an' God's Law : what David sees intil
> them baith : what mony might see forby, an
> they leuk in his e'en "

The 54th. Psalm which begins (A.V.) "Save me, O God, by thy Name, and judge me by thy strength," has this plaintive refrain :—

> " David uncolie worried an' harried flings
> the weight o' a' ontil God "

At the beginning of each Psalm, we are informed who wrote it : in such words as :—

> " Ane heigh-lilt o' David "
>
> or
>
> " Ane heigh-lilt o' Asaph's "

and for the anonymous writers we have the somewhat curt statement :—

> " By Wha's No Said."

The first Bible printed in Scotland was :—

THE BASSANDYNE BIBLE OF 1579.

The title page has these words : "The Bible and Holy Scriptures contained in the Old and Newe Testament, translated according to the Ebreu and Greek, and conferred with the best translations in divers languages. With most profitable annotations upon all the hard places of the Holy Scripture, and other things of grete importance, mete for the godly reader."

The Bassandyne Bible is stated to have been printed in Roman type, at Edinburgh, by Thomas Bassandyne, *cum privilegio :* which privilege assumed the practical form of a payment to the Crown "of the soume of twa hundreth pundis, money of this Realm."

The General Assembly ordered that every parish in Scotland should purchase a copy of this Bible, at the price of five pounds. But there was so little demand for the book, that the Privy Council made an order inflicting a penalty of £10 upon "every householder worth three hundred marks of yearly rent, and all substantious yeomen and burgesses, esteemed as worth £500, in land and goods, who did not possess a Bible in the vulgar tongue. They also appointed searchers or inquisitors to go from house to house, to see that such householders had provided themselves with Bibles.

And as it was found that the same Bible was made to do duty for more than one house, the searchers were empowered, "to require the sicht of the Bible, to see that it be marked with their own name, for eschewing of fraudulent dealing in that behalf."

The Magistrates and Town Council of Edinburgh also commanded all householders to purchase Bibles under severe pains and penalties, and informed them where they were "sauled."

Wycliffe's Bible.

Circa 1382-3.

John Wycliffe—whose name (spelt in diverse ways) is one of the highest value in English history—was born in Yorkshire about 1325.

Of the history of his youth, little is known, and he first came into public knowledge as Master of Balliol College, Oxford. But he soon retired from his mastership to a college living, and in 1374 was presented by the Crown to the Rectory of Lutterworth, in Leicestershire, where he died and was buried. He was a strong opponent of the Papal power: he denied the priestly power of absolution, the system of enforced confession, and the doctrines of penance and indulgences.

He appealed to the people in their own language and began his translation of the Bible, of which, as yet, there was no complete English version.

The characteristic of his teaching was its insistence on inward religion, in opposition to the outward rules and ceremonies which hampered the creed of the Roman Church.

But he brought the wrath of Holy Church down upon himself at last, by assailing the fundamental doctrine of transubstantiation, for which he was called to account by the convocation at Oxford and by the Council of the Archbishop of Canterbury, but he died shortly afterwards in 1384 and was buried at Lutterworth.

Thirty years after his death, forty-five articles, extracted from Wycliffe's writings, were condemned as heretical by the Council of Constance, which ordered the bones of the heretic to be dug up and burned, a sentence executed thirteen years later.

Wycliffe's Bible, A.D. 1383, is the most interesting example we have of our early English at the time when the different dialects were undergoing the process of unification. The three principal dialects of early English were:

(1) The Northumbrian, spoken in the district lying between the Humber and the Clyde, which district at that time bore the name that is now confined to one portion only, the County of Northumberland. This dialect is perhaps best preserved in what is now called Lowland Scotch, of which the strongest examples are to be found in the poems of Robert Burns, and of James Hogg, the Ettrick Shepherd, and in the prose writings of Sir Walter Scott, and the pleasant pages of the "Noctes Ambrosianæ" of Christopher North."

(2) The Midland was in use in the country lying between Northumbria and the Thames.

(3) The Southern, spoken in all the counties South of the Thames, in Somersetshire, Gloucestershire, and parts of Herefordshire and Worcestershire.

The Midland dialect finally prevailed in literature and usage, and it was in this dialect that Wycliffe wrote his Bible; although, as he was born in Yorkshire, we occasionally find Northumbrian words.

The spelling of this dialect (says Professor Skeat) was phonetic; as the word was spelt so it was pronounced. He also notices in Wycliffe's diction the use of familiar words in an obsolete sense, and instances amongst others :—*Take* for give; *chimnie* for furnace; *cofynes* for baskets; *eddrie briddis*, literally adders birds in the sense of adders' broods;

catel for goods and chattels; *sad* in the sense of firm, &c., &c.

But there are many other interesting examples of the change of the orthography and diction of our language that might be given. The following are mostly taken from the Gospels: "Taken an aunsewere in sleep" is rendered in our modern version, "warned of God in a dream."

Toun, or Town as we now spell it, is there used for a farm or field (St. Luke xiv., 18.), its original Scandinavian meaning:—"The first seide Y have bought a *toun* and Y have nede to go out and see it." Walter Scott retained this usage in the Lowland Scotch dialect of Andrew Fairservice (*Rob Roy*). "Where there's nae leddy about the *toun* (farm) to count the apples."

Clepe and *cleped* are used for call and called:

> "Fro Egypt have I *clepid* my son,"
> "And he shall be *clepid* a Nazarey."

Where the Authorised Version gives 'Repent ye' Wycliffe says, "Do ye penaunce." *Sour dough* is used for 'leaven,' and *Therf* for 'unleavened bread,' *Knygthis* for 'soldiers,' *Mesels* for 'lepers', *Castel* for 'a town or village,' and *Hei* (hay) or *heye* for 'grass.'

"Make alle men sitte to mete, bi cumpanyes on green *heye.*" St. Mark vi., 39.

Deem was generally used for 'judge,' and is still retained in the title of the Manx Judge—the Deemster. A good example of the use of this word is to be found in St. Matthew vii., 1. "Nile ye *deme,* that ye be not *demed;* for in what *doom* ye *demen,* ye schulen be *demed.*" In the Authorised Version the text runs:—Judge not that ye be not judged. For with what judgment ye judge, ye shall be judged." In several places Wycliffe uses *Christ* or *Crist* in the general sense of 'anointed.'

"Doing mercy to his *crist* David (to his anointed, to David. A.V.) Ps. xviii., 51. "Nyle ye touch my *cristis* (mine anointed) Ps. cv., 15.

Yvel at ese and *mal ese* are the quaint, though good, expressions for 'sick'; and *disease* is used in the sense of 'trouble' or 'annoyance' :—

"Comaunder (Master), the puple thristen and *diseasen* thee." St. Luke viii., 46. There is a curious expression in the same chapter :

"And had spendid al hir *catel in leeches*" (money on doctors).

In many texts in Wycliffe's Bible we find the word *Gess* (guess) used in the sense of 'think' or 'suppose,' as it is used colloquially to-day in the United States. Few phrases are in more frequent use across the water than the Yankee 'I guess.'

"Symount answered and seide, Y gess! that he to whom he forgaf more." St. Luke vii., 43.

"For thei gessen that thei ben herd in her (their) myche speeche." St. Matt. vi., 7.

"Who gessist thou is grittir in the Kyngdom of hevenes ?" St. Matt. xviii., 1.

Drench formerly meant to drown, and was so used by old writers down to the time of Chaucer and Wycliffe. It occurs in the 'Millere's Tale' (v. 3616) of *The Canterbury Tales*.

"Noe's flood comen walwing as the sea
To *drenchen* Alison."

In the passage in Wycliffe's Bible describing Peter walking on the water we find :—

"And whanne he began to *drench*, he cried and saide Lord make me saaf." St. Matt. xiv., 30.

In another gospel there is a very curious use of this word :—

"Thou schalt be *drenchid* til in to helle." (Thou shalt be thrust down to hell. A.V.) St. Luke x., 15.

Drowning in fire seems to us a curious and complicated metaphor.

Amongst other words used by Wycliffe, and now obsolete or changed in signification, may be noticed— *Biriel,* a tomb.

"And when the bodi was takun, Joseph lappide it in a clene sendel (cloth), and leide it in his new birial that he had hewun in a stoon." St. Matth. xxvii, 60.

Flom, a stream or river : 'And thei weren baptised of hym in the flom Jordan.' St. Mark i, 5.

Margarite, the Greek word for pearl : 'Nether caste youre Margaritis bifore swyne.' St. Matth. vii, 6.

Meyne, the old English word for household or attendants : 'If thei han cleped the hosbonde man Belsabub, hou mych more hys household meyne ?' St. Matth. x, 25. 'Whom the lord ordained on hys meyne.' St. Matth. xxiv, 46. 'They summoned up their meiny—straight took horse.' *King Lear,* Act 2, Sc. 4.

Queerne, a mill or millstone : 'Twey wymmen schulen be gryndying in o queerne.' St. Matth. xxiv, 41.

Frendesse, a female friend : *Spousesse,* a bride : *Lomb* and *Lambren,* lamb and lambs. *Lambren* was the old plural for lamb, taking the Saxon form ending in en, (instead of the French in s.) Amongst the few words that still retain the Saxon plural termination may be mentioned *oxen, brethren,* and *children. Eyen,* for eyes, and *sisteryn* for sisters, were in common use formerly, but have died out. *Volatiles,* birds. 'And axe thou volatiles of the air.' Job xii, 7.

Herborles, harbourless.

'I was herborles, and ye herboriden me.'

(I was homeless and ye lodged me)

'I was a stranger, and ye took me in.'   A.V.

St. Matth. xxv, 36.

This is a very noteworthy instance of the change in the meaning of words. The primary meaning of *harbour,* in the present day, is a place of shelter for ships: but it originally meant 'soldiers' quarters.' It was derived from the A.S. *heri,* an army, and *bergen,* a lodging.

The root *heri* still remains in Hereford, the ford of the army, and Harrogate, the road or way of the army. It is also found in Harbinger, the forerunner, the man who went in front to provide billets for the soldiers; and in Herring, the *army* fish, so called from the immense hosts in which it travels.

In the Genevan Bible we find the word in the form of Harbourous:

'Be ye *harbourous* (hospitable) one to another.' 1st. Peter iv, 9.

Chaucer uses the word in several forms:

Herbergage, an old French word for lodging: 'Upon this argument of Herbergage.' Prologue to the 'Coke's Tale.'

Herbergeours, harbingers, providers of lodging: 'By *Herbergeours* that wenten him before.'

"The Man of Lawe's Tale," 5415.

Herberwe, an Inn:

> ' I saw not this year, swiche a compagnie
> At once in this *herberwe*, as is now.'
>
> *Canterbury Tales.* Prologue.

Hereward the Wake, the 'Last of the English,' is a name well known in our history, and *Herepath*, the army path, still survives as a family name.

We find also the old English word *Broc* for badger:

'They wenten aboute in *broc* skynnes, and in skynnes of geet (goats) , nedi, angwis-ched and turmentid.'

> Hebrews, xi, 37.

Leep, a basket. This word is still in use locally in the form of bee-leep or beehive:

'But his disciples token him bi night, and leeten him doun in a *leep* by the wall.' Deeds (Acts) ix, 27.

Wycliffe uses frequently the quaint expression—'litel man of wit,' where we have *simple* in the Authorised Version :—

'A litel man of wit schal be the wisere.' Wyc.
'The simple is made wise.' A.V., Prov. xxi, 11.
Nol, the head :

'With hard *nol* (stiff-necked, A.V.) and uncircumsided hearts." Deeds, vii, 51.

In the form of *noule* it is used in this sense by Spenser:
'For yet his *noule* was totty (dizzy) of the must
Which he was treading in the wine vats.'

> *Fairie Queene*, 7, 7, 39.

Must was the old word for new wine, and is used by Wycliffe: 'For these men ben full of must.' Deeds, ii, 14.

Thewes, for manners :
'Nyle ye be disseyved, for evil speechis distrien good

thewes.' (Evil communications corrupt good manners. A.V.). I. Cor., xv, 34.

> 'As fele thede, as fele thewes.'
> (As many lands, as many customs).
>
> *Proverbs of Hendyng,* A.D. 1307.

Ether (either), is constantly used in this version for 'or,' as:

> 'Go to the ant ether pissemire.' Prov. vi, 6.

These are a few of the many instances that might be given, of the change in our language since Wycliffe's Bible first began to fix its etymology. It is also to be remarked that the book called in our Authorised Version 'The Acts of the Apostles' is headed in Wycliffe's Version 'Deeds of Apostles,' and 'Revelations' is called the Apocalypse.

The spelling of the names of persons and places in Wycliffe's Bible is sometimes very peculiar. For instance, the name of Pontius Pilate is found in the form of 'Pilat of Pounce,' 'Levi of Alphi' represents Levi, son of Alpheus, Simon Peter is spelt 'Symount Petir,' and Judas Iscariot 'Iudas Scarioth.' Gethsemane is hardly to be recognised in the word *Jessamanye* or Lama Sabacthani in *Lamaza batany.*

It is to Wycliffe that we largely, in fact principally, owe the consolidation of the various dialects existing in his time in England into one, and that, almost our present, language. No better example of the gradual but great change that has taken place in the English language could be given, than the comparison of the Lord's Prayer as it was written in the time of King Alfred (A.D. 871—901) with the Lord's Prayer 500 years later in Wycliffe's Bible, and of that again with the same prayer in the Authorised Version of 1611, which is in the same language as that of the Revised Version of 1885.

The Lord's Prayer in the time of King Alfred:

Uren Fader dhic art in heofnas
Our   Father which art in Heaven

Sic gehalged dhin noma
Be   hallowed   Thy   name

To cymedh dhin ric
Come Thy kingdom

Sic dhin willa sue is in heofnas and in eardhs
Be Thy   will so as in heaven and in earth

Vren hlaf ofer wirthe sel us to daeg
Our   loaf over substantial (?) give us to-day

And forgef us scylda urna
And forgive us debts ours

Sue we forgefan sculdgun vrum
As   we forgive   debtors ours

And no inleadh vridk in costung
And not inlead   us   in temptation

Als gefrig vrich fro ifle
But free   us   from evil

It may be noticed in this version of the Lord's Prayer that the concluding sentence " For thine is the kingdom and the power and the glory for ever. Amen " is omitted. It appears in the Authorised Version of the Bible (1611) in the Gospel of St. Matthew, but is not given by St. Luke. It was also omitted from both gospels by the New Testament Company in their Revised Version of 1885.

It is interesting to compare this version of Alfred's era with the Lord's Prayer in Wycliffe's Bible as it shows the gradual formation of a common tongue, and the extinction of the *patois* or provincial dialects which at one time were almost distinct languages.

The Lord's Prayer in Wycliffe's Bible, A.D. 1380.

Our Fadir that art in hevenes
Halewid be thi name ;
Thi kingdom come to ;

Be thi will done in earth as in hevene ;
Gyve to us this dai oure breed
    oure other substance ;
And forgive to us oure dettis ;
As we forgyven to oure dettouris ;
And lede us not into temptacioun ;
But delyvere us fro yvel.

             Amen.

The Lord's Prayer in Tyndale's time (A.D. 1526) had assumed very nearly the form it bears in our Authorised Version :—

O our father which arte in heven, halowed be thy name. Let thy kingdom come. Thy will be fulfilled, as well in erth, as hyt ys in heven. Geve us this daye oure dayley breade. And forgeve us our treaspases, even as we forgeve them which treaspas us. Leede us not into temptacion, but delyvre us from yvell. Amen.

Another interesting example of the changes in our language is cited by Mr. Halliwell, who gives the Apostles' Creed in the early Kentish dialect :—

Ich leve me God, fader almiti, makere of hevene and of erthe, and in Jesu Crist his sone *on lepi* oure Lord, that ikend is of the holi gost, ybore of Marie mayde, ypined under Pouns Pilate, ynaled a rode, dyad, and be-bered, yede doun to helle, thane thridde daye aros vram the dyade, stead tohevenes, zit a the right *half* of God the vader almiti, thannes to comene he is to deme the quike and the dyad. Ich yleve me the holi gost, holi cherche generalliche, mennesse of halzen, lesnesse of sennes, of vlesse arising, and lyf everlastinde. Zuo be hit.

Right *half* for right *side* occurs frequently in the older translations.

On lepi used above is an old word, meaning 'single.'

" An lepi blissa," (Our only bliss) "The Soul's Ward,"
v. 170.

The intervals of time between King Alfred and Wycliffe, and between Wycliffe and the writers of the present day are about the same—500 years, and it is worthy of remark that during the first epoch the language of England changed so greatly that the Lord's Prayer of Alfred and that of Wycliffe might have been written in two distinct tongues ; but that in the second period the language has remained almost the same, and the words of Wycliffe are even at this day "understanded of the people."

And the reason of this is, as already stated, that it was Wycliffe himself who, more than any other writer in English history, contributed to fix the spelling and pronunciation of our words ; and this was principally through his translation of the Bible which, although only a translation of a translation (being based on the Latin Vulgate of Jerome, A.D. 385) was the first complete version of the Scriptures given to our country in the language of its people about A.D. 1383.

Wycliffe's Bible, although presented only in manuscript, was largely circulated, and perhaps the care required in the copying, contributed to preserve uniformity in spelling.

However, shortly after his death came the invention of printing, and in 1483, about a century later, was born William Tyndale destined to produce the first printed copy of the New Testament in English—the foundation of all versions since published—and to fix substantially the spelling of the English language for all time.

To Chaucer, to whom Spenser in *The Fairie Queene,* refers as :—

"That old Dan Geffrey in whose gentle sprite,
The pure well-head of poesy did dwell,"

and to Gower we owe the formation of our tongue, and to Wycliffe and Shakespeare its perfection. Chaucer and Gower may have hewn the stone, but Wycliffe and Shakespeare carved the statue.

Wycliffe's Bible was our first entire Bible in English. How far this translation may be ascribed to Wycliffe's personal labours, is not accurately known, but the greater part of the New Testament, and part of the Old, are from his pen.

His friend, Nicholas de Hereford, is responsible for the first part of the Old Testament, down to the book of Baruch, of which the manuscript is in the Bodleian Library. But as the entrance of the Holy Land was denied to Moses, so it was not granted to Wycliffe to realise the desire of his life, the complete translation of the Bible into the English tongue.

But it was accomplished soon after his death by his faithful friend John Purvey, one of the leaders of the Lollards, " with mych travaile and with the ayde of diverse felawis and helperis," about 1390. A valuable reprint was issued from the Clarendon Press in 1879, and another of the Books of Job, the Psalms, Proverbs, and Solomon's Song in 1881, under the direction of that most erudite philological scholar, the Autocrat of Words, Professor Skeat.

Of this Bible, says Mr. Hoare, It is the " provocatio ad populum " of our first Reformer. It is the dying legacy of the sturdiest fighter of the day to the people of England. It is from the hand of the father of English prose, it embodies the great principle that the Bible is the People's Book and should speak the language of the People." Wyckliffe, like all strong men, was before his day, but as an old English saw has it " Strong men and water cleave their way."

Although this Version is generally called "Wycliffe's" it is really the work of three men :—himself and his friend Nicholas de Hereford, who made the translation about A.D. 1381, and John Purvey who revised it some seven or eight years later.

As a translation, says Mr. Hoare, it is a noble work, but it lacks uniformity of style, and is of very uneven merit, the result probably of the three collaborators. The diction is homely, rugged, and primitive, for our language was then only in the *process of formation ;* and the expressions often are of refreshing naïvety and quaintness. But whatever its defects or imperfections, and although it may lack the grace of Tyndale and the melody of Coverdale we can never forget that it is

OUR FIRST AND OLDEST BIBLE.

Tyndale's Bible.

A.D. 1536.

WILLIAM TYNDALE was born about A.D. 1484 at Berkeley, in Gloucestershire, and after many vicissitudes, much labour in his holy work, and remorseless persecution, was in the 52nd. year of his life, strangled at Vilvoorde Castle in the Low Countries, on the 6th. October, 1536, and his body subsequently burnt at the stake by order of the Council of Brabant.

Tyndale for some years studied at Magdalen College, Oxford, but migrated to Cambridge to profit himself by the wisdom of Erasmus, a Dutchman, at that time Professor of Greek in that University.

It was for the New Testament of Erasmus that the Vulgate was set aside, although Erasmus himself remained in communion with the Church of Rome. Of this translation Froude says:—"For the first time the laity were able to see, side by side, the Christianity which converted the world; and the Christianity of the Church, with a Borgia Pope, cardinal princes, ecclesiastical courts, *and a mythology of lies.*"

THE EFFECT WAS TO BE A SPIRITUAL EARTHQUAKE.

For some years Tyndale carried on his cherished pursuit of translating the Bible—first in the quiet repose of his chaplainship in the family of Sir John Walsh, at Sodbury, in Gloucestershire, and afterwards in the house of Humphrey of Monmouth, a wealthy merchant and alderman of London. But persecution still pursued him, and finding, to quote his own words, "That not only there was no room in my Lord of London's Palace to translate the New Testament, but also that there was no place to do it *in all England,*" he sought shelter at Hamburg in 1524.

In this retreat, in spite of opposition and persecution, he is supposed to have put into circulation some 30,000 printed copies of the New Testament, and a few years afterwards William Tyndale, "to whom may be justly assigned a place amongst the great ones of the earth," died by the hands of his persecutors.

Between the time of John Wycliffe and that of William Tyndale the art of printing was discovered, and in A.D. 1526 Tyndale produced the first *printed* New Testament in English. Of the Old Testament Books he translated only the Pentateuch, the Historical Books, and part of the Prophets.

In another respect TYNDALE'S BIBLE differed from all the English versions that preceded it. All of these were translations of the Latin Vulgate, itself a translation. Tyndale for the first time consulted such Hebrew and Greek MSS. as were accessible in his time. Every succeeding version is little more than a revision of Tyndale's; even our present Authorised Version owes to him the ease, beauty and strength for which it is so much admired. "The peculiar genius," says Mr. Froude, "which breathes through the English Bible, the mingled tenderness and majesty. the Saxon simplicity, the grandeur, unequalled, unapproached in the attempted improvements of modern scholars—all are here, and bear the impress of the mind of one man, and that man, William Tyndale."

Although the language of Tyndale's Bible is modern English in comparison with that of Wycliffe, it contains many quaint expressions :—

"And the Lord was with Joseph, and he was a *luckie felowe*" (a prosperous man), Gen. xxxix, 2.

"When ye praye, *bable* not moche as the gentyls do" (use not vain repetitions), St. Matthew vi, 7.

"Be not as lords over the *parrishes*" (God's heritage), 1 Peter v, 3.

"He let it forth to *fermers* (husbandmen), Luke xx, 9.

"Brought oxen and garlands to the *churchporch*" (gate), Acts xiv, 13.

"The rulers of the synagogue sent to them after the *lecture*" (reading of the law), Acts xiii, 15.

"When they had *said grace*" (sung a hymn), St. Matthew xxvi, 30.

"He sent forth the *hangman*" (executioner), St. Mark vi, 27.

"I was in the Sprete on a *Sondaye*" (the Lord's Day), Rev. i, x.

"Why did the hethen *grudge*?" (rage), Acts iv, 25.

"And every man went into his owne *shire toune* (city) to be taxed." St. Luke ii, 3.

"The whole neade not the *visicion*" (physician), St. Matt. ix, 12.

"Thou shalt find a piece of *twelve pens*" (money), St. Matt. xvii, 27.

"The day that followeth *Good Friday*" (*the Preparation* A.V.) St. Matt. xxvii, 62.

"All men *cannot away with* (receive) that saying," St. Matt. xix, 11.

"Thou shalt not *breake wedlocke* (commit adultery), St. Matt. xix, 18.

"Ye which have followed me in the second generation" (regeneration), St. Matt. xix, 28.

"I was *herbroulesse* (a stranger) and ye lodged me" St. Matt. xxv, 35.

"Be ye *herbrous* (hospitable), and that without grudginge," 1 Peter iv, 9.

"After three days shalbe *ester*" (passover), St. Matt. xxvi, 2.

"For we are not as many are, which *choppe and chaunge* (corrupt) the word of God." 2 Corinthians ii, 17.

"Butt the *mynisters* (servants) which drue the water knew." St. John ii, 9.

"Won beyng of them selves, which was a *poyet* (prophet) of their own." Titus i, 12.

The text that ends the marriage service in our Liturgy:

" and are not afraid with any amazement "
is rendered by Tyndale :—

"And be not afraid of every shadow." 1 Peter iii, 6.

We find also the somewhat curious expression of *seeing a sound* :—

"And I turned bake to see the voice that spake to me." The Revelacion of St. Jhon i, 12; and this phrase is perpetuated in the Authorised and the Revised Versions.

Of "shall be" Tyndale makes one word—shalbe, and he disguises the word "weightier" in the elaborate garb of "waygthyer" (St. Matt. xxiii, 23). "Anything" is spelt "entinge" in the following chapter, and we also find "tinke" for "think," "vysselles" for "vessels," and many other curiosities of spelling.

Tyndale uses the Saxon word "love" in place of the Greek "*charity*" which is found in the Authorised Version. "Now abideth fayth, hope and love, even these thre, but the chief of these is love." 1 Cor. xiii, 13. And again 1 Peter iv, 8, "For love (charity) covereth the multitude of sins." Also 1 Cor. 13, 4, "Love suffereth longe and is corteous," which in the Authorised Version is rendered "Charity suffereth long and is kind." It seems a pity that

the Saxon word was not retained; it would have avoided
the mistaken idea that the primary Christian virtue to which
the Apostle refers was *the giving of alms*, to which the
word charity is almost entirely restricted in our modern
usage.

Most biographical notices of Tyndale, says Mr. Dore,
are taken from John Foxe's Acts and Monuments of
Martyrs, but no reliance can be placed on the truth of any
uncorroborated statement made by Foxe.

Had this martyrologist been an honest man, his care-
lessness and credulity would have incapacitated him from
being a trustworthy historian. But, unfortunately, he was
not honest; he tampered with the documents that came
into his hands, and freely indulged in those very faults of
suppression and equivocation for which he condemned his
opponents.

The only document known to exist now, in Tyndale's
own handwriting, is a quaint, but pitifully pathetic, appeal
to the clemency of the governor of the Castle of Vilvoorde,
where he was confined for a year and a half before his
Martyrdom. The letter was written in Latin, and thus
translated :—

"I believe, right honourable Sir, that you are not
ignorant of what has been determined concerning me, by
the Council of Brabant. Therefore I entreat your Lord-
ship, and that by the Lord Jesus, that if I am to remain
here during the winter, you will request the Procureur to
be kind enough to send me from my goods, which he has
in his possession, a warmer cap, for I suffer extremely from
cold in the head, being afflicted with a perpetual catarrh,
which is considerably increased in this damp cell. A
warmer coat also, for that which I have is very thin, also a

piece of cloth to patch my leggings; my overcoat has been worn out, my shirts are also worn out. He has a woollen shirt of mine, if he will be kind enough to send it. I have also with him leggings of thicker cloth for putting on above, also warmer caps for wearing at night.

I also wish his permission to have a candle in the evening, as it is wearisome to sit alone in the dark. But above all, I entrust and beseech your clemency, to be urgent with the Procureur, that he may kindly permit me to have my Hebrew Bible, Hebrew Grammar, and Hebrew Dictionary, that I may spend my time with that study.

And in return, may you obtain your dearest wish, provided always it be consistent with the salvation of your soul. But if *any other resolution* has been come to, concerning me, before the conclusion of the winter, I shall be patient, abiding the will of God. Whose spirit, I pray, may ever direct your heart. Amen:

W. TYNDALE.

"The other resolution" (his death) had already been "come to" by the Council of Brabant, and in the autumn of 1536 the noblest and purest character on the long roll of English Martyrs, met the death he did not fear to face.

Coverdale's Bible.

1535.

In A.D. 1535 came the Bible of Myles Coverdale, sometime Lord Bishop of Exeter, who first translated the *whole* Bible into English. It was printed at Zurich, and dedicated to Henry VIII. This Bible, unlike Tyndale's, was not taken from the Hebrew and Greek MSS., but was, as stated in the Preface, "Faithfully and truly translated out of Douche (Dutch) and Latin into English, by your Grace's humble servant and daily oratour, Miles Coverdale."

MILES COVERDALE, "the most melodious of our translators" and one of the most striking characters in the noble band who gave God's word to his people, was Yorkshire born, as was John Wycliffe. He was born in 1488 and educated at the Augustinian Convent at Cambridge, "the head of which at that time was Dr. Robert Barnes, "*who bore his faggot*" in 1526.

Subsequently in 1527 Coverdale joined the Reformers, and became the intimate friend of Thomas Cromwell, and it is supposed that it was by the aid of Cromwell's purse that Coverdale pursued the compilation of the Great Bible of 1539.

He died in 1569, aged 81, and was buried in the Chancel of S. Bartholomew's Church, and when that Church was destroyed his bones were taken to the Church of S. Magnus.

Coverdale's translation of the Bible is one of singular grace and terseness, and of strength and simplicity of expression. It is in many respects one of the most interesting versions we have.

"This translation," says Mr. Hoare, in the Nineteenth Century, "is one of particular grace and power. There could scarcely be a greater contrast between two men than there is between Coverdale and Tyndale. If the latter be the Hercules of our biblical labourers, the former is certainly the Orpheus. Diffident and retiring in disposition, of delicate susceptibility, of great literary dexterity and resource, with a wonderful ear for cadence and rhythm, it is to Coverdale we owe much of that beautiful music which seems to well up out of the perennial springs of our Authorised Version."

" Coverdale stands in relation to Tyndale as gentleness does to strength, pliability and grace to robustness, and vigour, and modesty to self-confidence. He was to Tyndale as the ivy to the oak."

Coverdale's Bible is, in some respects, one of the most interesting versions we have, and a very excellent reprint from the copy in the library of the Duke of Sussex was published by Samuel Bagster, in 1838.

This Bible is sometimes called "The Treacle Bible," as in Jeremiah viii, 22, the sentence that in our version runs:—"Is there no balm in Gilead?" is there translated, "Is there no *triacle* at Galaad?" It is somewhat singular that in the Welsh Bible also, first translated by Dr. Morgan, Bishop of St. Asaph in 1588, the word "triacle" is used instead of balm : " *Onid oes driagl yn Gilead?*"

"Treacle" was formerly the word used for a medicament, compounded as an antidote against poisons and the bites of wild beasts: Lat. *Therica*, French *Theriaque*, M. E. *Triacle*, a sovereign remedy (Skeat).

Tryakyll, as a drug, is mentioned by Gawin Douglas, A.D. 1513 :—

"Tryakyll, druggis or electuary."
                    Prologue to 12th. Buk of Eneados.

Triacle is also used by Chaucer in the sense of a sovereign remedy :—

"Crist, which that is to every harm *triacle.*"
            "Man of Lawe's Tale." Prologue v. 4899.

The Douay Version of this text runs :—"Is there no *rosin* in Gilead ?"

Amongst the peculiarities of this Bible it may be mentioned that the Bishop calls the Books of Chronicles "Paralipomenon" (or things omitted—the Supplement), Solomon's Song, "Salamon's Balettes," the Lamentations of Jeremiah he calls "Treni" (Welsh *trueni*, misery), and he places Baruch amongst the Canonical Books. He also gives us "The Chapters in the Boke of Hester which are not found in the text of the Hebreu, but in the Greke and Latyn."

Amongst other curious expressions in this Bible we find :—

"What *felowe* is the Lorde ?" (Who is the Lord ?) Prov. xxx, 9.

"Arise, Barak, and *catch him that catcheth thee*" (Arise, Barak, and lead captivity captive. A.V.) Judges v, 12.

"As for Reuben, he stood hye *in his owne consayte.*" (Great thoughts of heart. A.V.) Judges v, 15.

"With the voice of thy *whystles*" (waterspouts), Ps. xli, 7.

"The dove bare an olive leafe in her *nebbe*" (mouth). Gen. viii, 11.

"Neither is there *good stomacke* (courage) in any man." Jos. xi, 11.

"And break his *brain-panne*" (and all to brake his skull), Judges ix, 53.

"Their widows were not looked upon in the daily *hand-reaching*" (ministration), Acts vi, 1.

"And he made ten *kettels* (lavers), 2 Chron. iv, 6.

"Mourn all ye wyne *suppers*" (drinkers), Joel i, 5.

"And all the people *sawe* the thunder and the lightning." Ex. xx, 18.

(The same curious expression of "*seeing* thunder" is preserved in the Authorised Version).

"O taste and see how *friendly* (good) the Lord is." Ps. xxxiv, 8.

"Tyll the *Worthye* (Shiloh) come." Gen. xlix, 10.

"Let another take his *Bishopricke*" (office), Ps. cviii, 8.

And perhaps the most curious of all :—

"Thou shalt not be afraid of any *bugges* (terror) at night." Ps. xc, 5.

(The modern word is bogy, a goblin).

In the 6th Chapter of Numbers he used the word "absteyner" instead of "Nazarite" as in our version, and he constantly uses the word "hell" where we now have "grave":—

"Who shall give thee thanks in the hell?" Ps. vi, 4.

"Hell shall be their dwelling." Ps. xlviii, 14.

"Deliver my soul from the power of hell." Ps. xlviii, 15.

"They lie in the hell like sheep." Ps. xlviii, 15.

In all these verses, and many others where Coverdale uses the word "hell" the Authorised Version has "grave."

The spelling is sometimes very curious, as for instance, in what the Bishop calls "The second boke Regum" (our 2nd. Samuel) a verse runs :—

"And he saw a woman *waszshing* herself, and she was of a very fayre *bewty*."

Waszshing for "washing" is ingenious spelling, but the same thing occurs again in "huszbande," "buszshels," "guszhe," "baszkettes," and "wyszdome," which we now write more simply, husband, bushels, gush, baskets and wisdom. "Szkynne" takes a superfluity of letters for so simple a monosyllable as "skin."

The "Great Bible" of 1539, which might be perhaps more fittingly described as the Big Bible, was also principally the work of Miles Coverdale.

Matthew's Bible.

1537.

This Bible—the second printed version of the Bible in English—is supposed to have been the continuation of Tyndale's work by his friend John Rogers, whose name was suppressed on the score of prudence, and the name of Thomas Matthew—an unknown and doubtful personality—used as a mask to conceal the fact that the work was Tyndale's.

It appeared in 1537, as the first Royally authorised English Bible. It was not a new translation, but a composite book—made up of Tyndale's Pentateuch and New Testament—and the rest from Coverdale. It was remarkable for the excessive Lutheranisms of its annotations, and was the direct ancestor, through the Great Bible and the Bishops' Bible, of the Authorised Version of 1611.

Mr. Dore—in his laborious work on "Old Bibles," published by Eyre and Spottiswoode in 1888—gives extracts from the Act of Parliament which prohibited the circulation of Tyndale's translation and authorized that of Matthew, although Matthew's Bible is merely Tyndale's translation under another name.

It is to be regretted that the extracts are too long to be published *in extenso*—as they would more than repay the time occupied by the curious student of religious history in their perusal.

The Act was passed in the 34th. year of our most religious and gracious Sovereign King Henry VIII., a monarch who married six women, of whom he divorced two, and murdered two. The Act has the following comprehensive, but somewhat vague, heading :—

> "*An Act for the advauncement of true religion and the abolishment of the contrary.*"

In the preamble the King refers to "the *great libertie* granted to them (his subjects) in having amongst them, and in their hands, the old and new Testament," and proceeds to regret "the various arguments, tumults and scisms that have arisen thereout—amongst his said subjects —to the great displeasure of his Majestie, and contrary to his grace's true meaning, good intention, *and most godly purpose.*

For the reformation thereof, his Majesty most virtuously ordains "that all manner of books of the old and new testaments, in English, of the crafty, false and untrue translation of Tyndale, shall be forbidden to be kept or used in this realm, or other the King's dominion." The penalty for the first offence against the enactment is a fine of ten pounds (a large sum in those days) and for the second "he shall forfeit all his goodes, *and his body to be committed to perpetual prison.*" This clause also inflicts a fine of five pounds on anyone having in his possession a book maintaining "the *damnable* opinions of the Anabaptists," whose chief doctrine was adult Baptism.

The next section—although it might have been at the time vexatious—in the present day appears only humorous:—

All Bibles in England, not being of Tyndale's translations, are authorized. Nevertheless, "if there be found in such bible, any annotacions or preamble, then every person shall before the 1st. day of October next cutte or blotte the same, in such wise that they (the annotacions) cannot be read, under a penalty of forty shillings."

From these penalties are exempted, amongst other books, any entitled "the King's highness proclamations," Gower's books, and Chaucer's "*Canterbury Tales*," "unless the King's Majesty shall hereafter make special proclamation for the condemnacion of the same."

It was also graciously conceded "that all printers maye lawfully print all such books contayning *matters of religion* as the King's Majestie shall by his bill allow and aprove."

In another section of this Act his grace's magnanimity concedes to every nobleman and gentleman—being a householder—the privilege of reading "in his own house, orchards, or garden, any text of the approved Bibles, so the same be done quietly and without disturbance of good order."

To noble women and gentlewomen—this concession of liberty was somewhat restricted—they were permitted to read *to themselves alone*, and not to others—any texts of the said Bibles—anything in this Act to the contrary notwithstanding.

But for the lower orders it was enacted that after the first of July—no *women*, artificers, prentyses, serving-men, yeomen or labourers, shall read within this realm, or any other the King's dominyons, the Bible in English, *to himself or to any other, privately or openly*, upon payne of one month's imprisonment for every offence.

Such was the Law of England, in what we still call "The Good Old days."

The last issue of Matthew's Bible was by Nicholas Hyll, dwelling in Saynt John Street, and was published in 1557 "at the cost and charges of certain honest men of the same occupation (booksellers) whose names be on their bokes."

Taverner's Bible.

1539.

Of this Bible, a pirated copy of Matthew's, very little is known, and it is of no particular interest. It was printed at the sign of "The Sonne" by John Bydell for Thomas Bartlett, *cum privilegio*, and was dedicated to Henry VIII.

Taverner was born in 1505, and graduated at S. Benet's College, Cambridge, but migrated to Oxford to study classics. He was taken up by Thos. Cromwell, and although not in orders was granted a license to preach. Taverner's Bible appears to have been a single edition, and never took hold of the people. It ends with this note:—

"To the honour and prayse of God, was this Bible prynted and fynyshed in the year of our Lord and Saviour Jesu Crist MDLI. Imprinted at London by Jhon Daye, dwelling over Alders-gate beneath Saint Martyn."

Taverner's Bible was the first complete Bible published on English soil.

The Great Bible.

1539.

A revised edition of Tyndale's edited by Cranmer, was the first *Authorised* English Bible. It was printed in Paris under the superintendence of Coverdale. From this version the Psalms and other portions of the Bible contained in the Prayer Book are taken. This Bible was the first placed "by Authority" (of Queen Elizabeth) in the parish Churches of England.

The Great Bible for nearly thirty years held its place as the Standard Bible of England, and from 1539 to 1566 went through some ten editions. The second edition, A.D. 1540, with a preface by Cranmer, received the personal authorization of Henry VIII, and no new Version of the Bible was issued from the end of his reign till after the close of the Marian persecutions; under which John Rogers and Archbishop Cranmer were martyred and the Bishop of Exeter, Miles Coverdale, escaped death by exile.

In 1560 was issued

THE GENEVAN BIBLE,

long the favourite Bible of the Puritans. It had these distinctive peculiarities—It was the first Bible printed in the present Roman type. All the previous versions had been in black letter. It was also the first in which the chapters were divided into verses, and the first to omit the Apocrypha. It was familiarly known as "The Breeches Bible" from its rendering of Gen. iii, 7, where Adam and Eve "sewed fig tree leaves together and made themselves *breeches.*" (Aprons is the word used in the Authorised Version.) In this the Song of Solomon is called "An excellent Song which was Salomon's."

The Prayer of Manasseh, King of the Jews, now included in the Apocrypha, was placed among the Canonical Books.

A great feature of this Bible was its copious marginal notes, and it is to the dislike of James I. to their Puritanical, political and religious bias, that we owe, to a great extent, the production of our Authorised Version of 1611.

At the time when the proposition for a new translation was being discussed at the Hampton Court conference, King James said: "That he did not consider any translation into English that had been hitherto made to be satisfactory; but that the worst of all versions was the Genevan, some of the notes of which were partial, untrue, seditious, and savoured too much of dangerous and traitorous conceits."

One of the first rules made by the Company of translators of the Authorized Version was, that there should be no marginal notes except such as were necessary for the explanation of Hebrew and Greek words.

This one rule did more than anything else to make our authorized version the common Bible of all sects and classes of religion and politics in England.

The text of the Genevan Bible is, to all intents and purposes, the same as our own, with the exception of certain variations of diction and expression, and the use of some words that have since died out or have changed in signification.

An instance of the former is a verse that is given in our Authorised Version thus :

"Take therefore no thought for the morrow, for the morrow shall take thought of the things of itself. Sufficient unto the day is the evil thereof."

In the Genevan Bible it runs :

"Care not then for the morow for the morow shall care for it selfe. The day has enough with his owne grief."
—St. Matt. vi, 34.

Many instances might be given of the use of words that have changed in meaning :

In the Gospel of St. Mark v, 12, we find this passage :—

"And al the devils besought him saying, &c., and incontinently (forthwith) Jesus gave them leave."

Incontinently, now meaning intemperately or licentiously, is here used in the sense of immediately, and is so employed in *Othello*, Act I, Sc. 3.

Roderigo : "I will *incontinently* drown myself."

In this Bible, as in Wycliffe's, the old Anglo-Saxon word *to ere*, i.e., to plough, is used. The text that is rendered in our Version :

"He that ploweth should plow in hope."

appears in both these Bibles in exactly the same words:

"He that erith, owith to ere in hope." 1 Cor. ix, 10.

Another obsolete word found in both Bibles is *Disease* in the sense of trouble or annoy:

"Thy daughter is dead, why *diseasest* thou the master?" St. Mark v, 35.

"And she threw in two mites which make a *quadrin*" (farthing). Mark xii, 42.

"Nor swaddled in *clouts*." One of the few English words of Welsh origin, is still used in dish clout, Ezekiel xvi, 4.

"Teach a child in the *trade* of his way." Proverbs xxii, 6.

The Authorised Version reads "Train up a child in the way he should go." Trade, in the sense of path or track, is used locally in parts of England, and game-keepers speak of "the *trade* (or tread) of rabbits."

"And an hundred *frailes* (baskets) of raisins." 1 Sam. xxv, 13.

"By his *neesings* (sneezings) a light doth shine." Job xli, 18.

"We trussed up our *fardels*" (burdens), Acts xxxi, 15.

In Hamlet's great soliloquy—"To be or not to be," Act III, Sc. 1, he asks:—

"Who would fardels bear
To grunt and sweat under a weary life?"

The Authorized Version renders this passage, "We took up our *carriages*." The word carriage being used in the sense of what they carried, and not that which carried them, its present meaning.

We also find *Disdain* for displease, *beneficiall* for merciful, *avoyded* for emptying (When the priests *avoyded* the ashes), *chapman* for trafficker, *brast* for burst, *backe* for bat (the bird), *banket* for banquet, *fet* for fetch, *pill* for getting an advantage, *grinne* or *gryn* for a snare, and *grieces* for stairs (*Grees*, Wyc. Acts xxi, 35. Welsh, *grisiau*)—"And when Paul came to the *grees* (stairs) it befel that he was borun of knightes (soldiers) for strength of the people." We still retain the use of this word in the phrase "by de*grees.*" These are a few instances of the many words found in this Bible that have since changed in spelling or meaning, but there is no vital difference between the texts of the Genevan Bible and our own.

The Genevan Bible was principally translated by Nonconformists at Geneva, who fled there soon after the death of Edward the 6th. to escape the persecutions that arose under the rule of that Popish Sovereign, to be thereafter known to history, through all time, as " Bloody Mary."

Geneva was at that time so saturated with those doctrines of Calvin, which for a long period of the Puritan occupation of religion in England, " threatened the extinction of Christianity," that it was almost impossible for the translators to avoid being drawn away from the higher teachings of the Church of their Baptism.

The marginal notes were largely those of narrow sectaries, often bitter, more often incorrect, and not unfrequently immoral. A note to Matt. ii, 12, runs thus:— "Promes oght not (promises ought not) to be kept when the preaching of God's Truth is hindered." A somewhat dubious and dangerous exposition of morality, when we consider that they, the Puritans, had constituted themselves the sole and irresponsible judges of the question propounded, but not answered, by the jesting Pilate, "What *is* truth ?"

Another marginal note is an interesting instance of the

nature and quality of the Christian charity and brotherly love pervading the Puritan mind. It is at Rev. ix, 3: "Locusts are false teachers, with monks, friars, cardinals, archbishops, &c., which forsake Christ to maintain false doctrine." But the note that rankled most in the King's mind, remembering the sad fate of his beautiful, but unfortunate mother, was one in 2 Chron. xv, where it is recorded that Asa removed his mother from the throne, because she made an idol in a grove. The note runs:— "Herein he shewed that he lacked zeal, for she ought to have died." Another that gave grave annoyance to the didactic author of "The Counterblast" and "Eikon Basilike" was a comment on the conduct of the Egyptian midwives, in disobeying the commands of Pharoah, and concealing the men-children. The annotation approved their action and said that their disobedience to the King was lawful. This clashed with the proud Stuart theories of the divine right of kings to be above all law, and the indignant monarch exclaimed "It is false! to disobey a king is not lawful; such traitorous conceits should not go forth to the people."

A modern writer on this subject admonishes us to remember that the universal desire for a Bible in England, which we read so much of in religious publications, is more than doubtful.

So far from England being a "Bible-thirsty land" there was no desire whatever for an English version at that time, excepting among a small minority of the people.

At any rate, as regards the versions anterior to King James's Bible of 1611 there was no great desire or demand, not merely among the clergy, but the great majority of the people, for a vernacular Bible. The universal desire for a Bible in England, which we see so often asserted in religious works existed only in the imagination of the writers.

It was found with even the Genevan version, the most extensively popular of all versions, that as in the case of all the early English Bibles it was much easier to print them than to sell them, there being very little desire on the part of the English people for a vernacular Bible.

It is a fact that in Scotland (as mentioned above) soon after the publication of the Bassandyne Bible in 1579, an Act was passed enforcing a penalty of ten pounds (Scotch) on everyone having an income of £500 a year, who did not purchase a copy of the Bible. It is probable that this want of desire to possess a Bible may have arisen in part from the fact that at that time comparatively few of the laity, and, probably many of the clergy, could have read the book, even if they had possessed a copy. Whatever the reason might have been, the fact remains that penal enactments were made to force it into circulation, and Royal Proclamations issued threatening the King's displeasure to those who neglected to purchase copies.

In 1568 was published

The Bishops' Bible,

or Parker's Bible, compiled by Archbishop Parker of Canterbury, and his brother bishops; and as the Geneva Bible was the Bible of the Puritans, so this was the favourite version of Holy Church.

The Anglo-Rhemish Version was a translation from the Latin Vulgate by Roman Catholics who objected both to the Genevan and Bishops' Bible. It was made and published at Rheims in 1582, from which place it takes its name.

Fancy Bibles.

Besides these well known and standard versions valuable to the student of the Bible, and the scholar of Anglo-Saxon, there have been certain versions that we may call "Fancy Bibles," which take their names from typographical errors or mistakes of expression, and have an artificial value for collectors of curiosities:—Amongst them may be mentioned

THE PRINTERS BIBLE:—In which by error, the word "Printers" was substituted for "Princes" in Psalm cxix, 161, "*Printers* have persecuted me without a cause."

THE WIFE'S BIBLE:—In Tyndale's New Testament of 1538, "Think on this *wise*," 2 Cor. x, 11, is made to read "Think on his *wife*."

THE WHIG BIBLE:—Being the second edition of the Genevan Bible 1562. In the Beatitudes, by a printer's error "Blessed are the *peace* makers" is converted into "Blessed are the *place* makers."

THE WICKED BIBLE, 1631:—The word "not" is omitted from the seventh commandment.

THE SERVANT BIBLE:—Now the *servant* (serpent A.V.) was more subtle than all the beasts of the field (Genesis iii, 1.)

THE JUDAS BIBLE:—Then cometh *Judas* (Jesus A.V.) and his disciples (Matthew xxvi, 36.)

THE PAGAN BIBLE:—Containing a woodcut of Mount Olympus and heathen gods.

THE VINEGAR BIBLE:—Genevan 1717. This word was substituted for "*Vineyard*" in the Parable that bears that name (Luke xx.)

THE BUGGE BIBLE:—Of Coverdale, so called from the rendering of the 5th. verse of Psalm xc, "Be not afraid of any *bugges* (modern bogy) by night."

THE BREECHES BIBLE:—The Genevan Bible is often called by this name as it uses this word instead of *aprons* in Genesis iii, 7.

THE TREACLE BIBLE:—Coverdale's Bible is also thus called, as he uses the word treacle instead of "balm" in Jeremiah viii, 2, "Is there no balm in Gilead?" A.V.

And the ROSIN BIBLE, the Douai Version of 1582 takes its name from the use of the word "rosin" in place of balm in the same verse.

There are several other Bibles such as the "He" and "She" Bibles, the "Standing Fishes," the "Ear to Ear," and the "Murderers" Bibles, and a strange printer's error occurs in all the copies of the Bishops' Bible, which contain the Prayer-Book Psalms. The 29th. verse of the 37th. Psalm reads, "*The righteous shall be punished;* as for the seed of the ungodly it shall be rooted out" in place of "the *unrighteous* shall be punished." But these "fancy" editions are of no increased value to anyone on account of their errors, save to the curiosity-monger.

But besides these "Fancy Bibles" which take their names from the curious or mistaken usage of one word or some slight typographical error, there remain in our authorised and revised versions many curious expressions and words, some of which are not known generally, and others of which although the meaning has been guessed at it has never been absolutely and accurately deciphered.

It might have been an Irish translator who presents us in Isaiah xxxvii, 36, with these words:—"And when they arose, early in the morning, they were all dead corpses."

In the Authorised Version appears in Isaiah vii, 20, a very curious expression which is perpetuated in the Revised Version and which runs thus :—

" In that day shall the Lord shave with a razor that is hired."

In Jeremiah vii, 18, occurs the phrase : "To make cakes to the Queen of Heaven, and to pour out drink offerings unto other Gods."

Isaiah xlvii, 7 : "And thou saidst, I shall be a *lady for ever*, so that thou didst not lay these things to thy heart."

Isaiah xiv, 8 : "No *feller* is come up against us."

Ezekiel x, 10 : "As if a wheel had been within a wheel."

In the Authorised Version, Jeremiah xxiv, 2, we have the expression : "a basket of very *naughty* figs." In the Revised Version it reads " very *bad* figs."

Jeremiah xliv, 17 : "To burn incense to the Queen of Heaven."

Amos vii, 7 : "And the Lord stood *upon* a wall *made by a plumbline*, with a plumbline in his hand.

2 Samuel xx, 16 : "Then cried a wise woman out of the city, " *Hear, hear.*"

Isaiah l, 7 : "I set my face like a *flint.*"

Jeremiah xxv, 27 : "Be drunken and *spue.*"

Isaiah iv, 1 : "And in that day seven women shall take hold of one man."

Isaiah i, 25 : "And will take away all thy *tin.*"

Ezekiel xxx, 2 : "Woe worth the day."

Isaiah v, 18 : "And draw sin as it were with a cart rope."

Isaiah vii, 18: "And the Lord shall *hiss for the fly,* that is in the uttermost parts of the rivers of Egypt."

Isaiah iii, 18: "In that day the Lord will take away the bravery of their *cauls*" [caps—SKEAT].

The instances of these "Curiosities of Biblical Literature" that are given here, are taken from the books of the prophets in which they principally abound, but they occur, as might be expected in a book written in the English of 300 years ago, in other Books of the Old Testament.

In the books of the prophets we find "For my sword shall be bathed in heaven," Isaiah xxxiv, 5, A.V. This text is written in the Revised Version:—"For my sword has drunk its fill in heaven," which does not render the passage less obscure."

"And the *satyr* shall cry to his fellow." Isaiah xxxiv, 14. Satyr was a sylvan god, half man and half goat, and the word is used here for a "he goat." It was this monster that Hamlet had in his mind when comparing his father and the uncle who murdered him :—

"Hyperion to a *satyr.*"—Act i, sc. 2.

There are many other expressions and words used in the Authorised Version of the Bible that are now obsolete or only in provincial use, but even a summary of them would weary both the reader and the writer.

At last in A.D. 1611 the combined wisdom of the divines and scholars of Oxford and Cambridge produced our present

Authorised Version.

A.D. 1611,

the most splendid example we have of the strength, the terseness, and the beauty of the English language. The Version of the Sacred Writings that is destined in all probability (the Revised Version of 1885 notwithstanding) to remain for ever the

BIBLE OF THE BRITISH PEOPLE.

It may be said here that the strength of the English Language, in all honest expression of feeling, whether of joy, sorrow, love, anger or pain, lies in those words of our composite tongue that are of Saxon origin, and that they are most copiously used by the best of our writers.

But, says a recent writer on this subject, the predominance of Saxon in the Authorised Version of the Bible is very remarkable. As compared with Latin words, the Saxon actually constitute some nine-tenths of the book. In Shakespeare the proportion is approximately eighty-five per cent., in Swift's writings it is ninety, in Johnson seventy-five, and in Gibbon seventy. In the Lord's Prayer of the Authorised Version, fifty-nine words out of sixty-five are Saxon.

In 1604 a conference of Bishops and clergy was held in Hampton Court Palace, under the presidency of James I. himself, to consider the defectiveness of the current translations of the Bible, with a view to emendation.

At this date there were three different versions of the Bible circulating in England :—

I.—THE GENEVAN BIBLE of 1560 (otherwise called the Breeches Bible) which ran through about sixty editions between that date and 1644. This was the favourite Bible of the people, and had by far the largest circulation.

Between its publication and the Civil War no less than one hundred and sixty editions passed into circulation. But it was saturated with the narrowest doctrines of Calvin, it became the household Bible of Scotland, and left that country steeped in the stern uncompromising Puritanism, which grafted the vindictive passions of the old Judaical dispensation on the soft teaching of the new Law of Love, the great inheritance of Christianity from Him :—

"Who stilled the rolling waves of Galilee."

II.—THE BISHOPS' BIBLE, A.D. 1586, (which ran through some twenty editions) otherwise called Archbishop Parker's Bible, took its name from the fact that the majority of the Revision Committee was taken from the Episcopal Bench.

It was the antithesis of the Genevan Bible, and therefore much cherished by Holy Church and had the support of Convocation, but this notwithstanding, it may justly be ranked with the poorest of the English translations.

"It was costly, it was cumbersome, its imposing appearance did not atone for its defects. It did not satisfy scholars, and it was ill suited to the general public; besides that, some of the illustrations were immodest, if not indecent."

The Bishops' Bible ran a course of about forty years, when it expired. The last copy bears date 1606.

III.—THE GREAT BIBLE of Henry.VIII, A.D. 1539, (which passed through 10 editions) "might at that time (1604) be seen chained to a stone or wooden post in many of the country parish churches."

It was for about thirty years the Standard Bible of the kingdom, and was sometimes attributed to Thomas Cranmer, Archbishop of Canterbury, who "bore his faggot" in 1556 during the Marian persecutions (or murders). Cranmer was no doubt intimately connected with its publication, and himself wrote the preface to the edition of 1540. This edition received King Henry the Eighth's personal authorisation.

The Great Bible was really little more than a revised edition of Tyndale. The version of the Psalms that appears in our "Common Prayer Book" and the sentences in the Communion Service are from the Great Bible. .

But none of these versions were likely to obtain general acceptance and satisfy at once the schoolmen and the sectaries. The Genevan, though a far more accurate, and possibly honest, translation than that over which Archbishop Parker presided, was so impregnated in its text and marginal notes with Calvinism and Puritanism as to have become the organ of the narrowest sectaries of the Cromwellian epoch and of the *Praise God Barebones* school.

The Great Bible, the bible of another Cromwell, and of Archbishop Cranmer, was unwieldy, expensive, and had fallen out of fashion, whilst the Bishops' Bible, impugned as least worthy of all the translations, had become the badge of the Church party, as had the Genevan Version of the Nonconformists.

This alone would have created a demand for a new version, which could be accepted in common by the rival religions, and we may also say, political parties. But the supply to that demand might not have come for many a long year, had it not been for the mixture of vanity, meanness and narrow-mindedness that contributed to form our first Stuart monarch James I. of England and VI. of Scotland, called by Sully "the wisest fool in Christendom."

James desired to add a new translation (dedicated to his high Puissance) to the glories of his reign, but even more, he desired to extinguish the popular, but to him obnoxious Genevan Bible, whose marginal notes, as stated before, cast doubt (amongst other things) on the divine right of Kings, and grievously vexed the soul of the Royal champion of the doctrine.

To the exercise of these by no means exalted attributes by James I., the people of England are largely indebted for their greatest literary glory and their noblest inheritance, the Bible of 1611. It is a stately monument (*œre perennius*) to the memory of those great and learned scholars who themselves erected it, it is a record of the arduous, faithful and loving labour of the most holy men of that age.

And beyond this, and also beyond its grace and beauty, unsurpassed in the literary history of the world, it is the Book of Books, and the noblest expression we have of

GOD'S MESSAGE TO MAN.

To a Roman Catholic Divine, Father Faber, we are indebted for the following graceful tribute to the excellence and beauty of the language of our version, as compared with the uncouthness of those of the Romanists:

"Who will say that the uncommon beauty and marvellous English of the Protestant Bible is not one of the great strongholds of heresy in this country?

"It lives on the ear like a music that can never be forgotten—like the sound of church bells, which the convert hardly knows how he can forego. Its felicities seem often to be almost things rather than words. It is part of the national mind, and the anchor of the national seriousness. Nay, it is worshipped with a positive idolatry, in extenuation of whose fanaticism its intrinsic beauty pleads availingly with the scholar. The memory of the dead passes into it. The potent traditions of childhood are stereotyped in its verses. The power of all the griefs and trials of a man is hidden beneath its words.

"It is the representative of his best moments. All that there has been about him of soft, and gentle, and pure, and penitent, and good, speaks to him for ever out of his English Bible.

"It is his Sacred Thing, which doubt has never dimmed, and controversy never soiled. In the length and breadth of the land there is not a Protestant with one spark of religiousness about him, whose spiritual biography is not in his Saxon Bible."

And for much, perhaps for most of this great legacy we owe a debt of ever-abiding gratitude to the memory of

WILLIAM TYNDALE.

The Revised Version.
1885.

Whether any Revision of a book that had occupied undisputed pre-eminence for nearly three centuries were required at all may well be questioned. The Bible of James I., although the text may not have been in some places structurally correct, was a book of such marvellous strength of language and beauty of diction, that it had taken root in the hearts of millions of men, not only where our own tongue is spoken, but in foreign countries and in the islands lying in far distant seas. The almost incredible way in which this version that we all know by the supreme title of "The" Bible has spread over the face of the civilized world, is evidenced by the facts that from one centre of distribution alone, The British and Foreign Bible Society, have been issued since 1804, the astounding number of 170,000,000 of copies, written in almost every language spoken by the nations of the world, and that the *annual* output of the English parent press exceeds four millions.

Was it probable that a book that had been disseminated in such incomprehensible numbers and with such lightning rapidity and penetration, into the hearts and homes of different speaking peoples, should be easily effaced?

Or that the Bible established in the affections of the childhood of millions of men, who had drawn in their love for it with their mothers' milk, should be replaced by another that might be of more correct grammatical construction, but in the process of development had lost much of the dignity as well as of the homely phraseology that appealed to their hearts, in the Old Book on which they were suckled?

At the time the Authorised Version of 1611 was contemplated, there were (as said above) other rivals for popular approval, but when the revision of it was suggested in 1870 by the Bishop of Winchester, Samuel Wilberforce, the Authorised Version had no rival: it stood alone, supreme and peerless. It had been read, it had been cherished, not only in the parish churches, but in the cottage-homes of England. It had become part of the daily life and daily worship of peer and peasant.

It had become gradually engraved on the hearts of a people who love their Bible with an almost idolatrous devotion. It formed part of their Common Prayer Book, which for strength, gravity and beauty of language, (more especially in the Collects) stands second only to THE BOOK itself, in the hearts of the many millions who are members of the National and Established Church of their country. Why then this desire to change or remove a force so strong and so deeply rooted?

It has been suggested that the discovery of the three Codices: the Alexandrian, the Vatican, and the last of all, the Sinaitic, only found in 1844, all of which were unknown to the translators of 1611, might add new light to the book descended from the Patriarchs, the Prophets and the Apostles, but whose pedigree could be traced no further back than the Septuagint and the Vulgate of S. Jerome.

But to the ordinary reader, and most of those who read the book may be thus described, this increase of our spiritual wealth does not seem to have accrued to us. The alterations, particularly in the New Testament, appear to be unimportant, unnecessary in many cases, and of doubtful value in all. The whole work seems to be the outcome of a desire to attain the perfection of grammatical accurary and literal reproduction of the text, at the sacrifice of the soft melody of the older, though possibly less accurate translation, a melody that from our cradle has rung in our ears as "the sound of the Church-going bell."

However this may be, the Bible of 1611 was not written as an object lesson to its readers in the construction of Greek particles. It was written to carry the divine message to the hearts of humanity, and it has done so. Why then this late revision and the new version, which even now in little more than a decade, has faded out of our remembrance?

In a recent work on the "Evolution of the Bible" the author, an eminent Balliol scholar, writing about the Revised Version, says :—

"If we may make bold to formulate a wish for the success of any future committee of Revisioners, it would be the wish that no microbe of the *Morbus Grammaticus* should ever affect them : and that they should never be persuaded to devote so disproportionate an amount of their sympathies to our scholarship and leave so little over to gratify our literary sensibilities.

"We trust that the Revisor of the future may be enabled to look to something beyond his Lexicon. We hold, in fine, the pious hope, that when next the Jerusalem Chamber is tenanted by a body of Revisors, they may never be haunted (like their last predecessors) by the ghost of the man who regretted with his dying breath *that he had not devoted the whole of his life to the dative case.*"

It may be supposed that the alterations in our old Bible by the Revisioners of 1885 have been satisfactory to themselves, or at least to some of them; but the new book was "caviare to the general." It was a blank cartridge. However, the Revisors of the Old Testament merit our thanks for two improvements. They divided the poetical books into proper lines, and they substituted "Sheol," a word we do not yet quite understand, for "hell," a word we have always misunderstood."

A noteworthy instance of the vexatious change of words that we have known so well and loved so long, occurs in the revised text of the last chapter of Ecclesiastes, one of the most graceful and pathetic of the Holy Writings, unsurpassed for poetic beauty, in a book that breathes in its pages the Divine Melody.

In the 5th. verse of that chapter, in its matchless metaphor of man's old age:—"In the day when the keepers of the house tremble, and the strong men bow themselves, and the grinders cease because they are few, and those that look out of the window are darkened": in that verse one line runs:—

"And desire shall fail."

. This is rendered by the Company of Revisioners, "And the caperberry shall fail." Wycliffe has "Capperis shall be distried" (destroyed). Coverdale avoids it, and substitutes "when great poverty shall break in." In the Genevan Bible it is rendered "And concupisence shall be driven away." Most people who understand the allusion would prefer the more graceful rendering of the older divines; and as the *Treacle*, the *Breeches*, and the *Printers* Bibles took their names from accidental words in those versions— if any further designation be wanted of this Bible than the " Revised Version," it might claim the proud title of

THE CAPERBERRY BIBLE.

In the reign of Henry III, in the famous Parliament of Merton, when the prelates endeavoured to impose some portion of the Roman Canon Law on the legislation of this country, all the Earls and Barons with one voice answered:—

" NOLUMUS LEGES ANGLIÆ MUTARE."

So at nearly the close of the third century of the reign of the old English Bible of the Stuart epoch, we, the people of England, say with equal loyalty and fidelity, that we desire no change in the words of the book that has soaked into the hearts of our childhood, as the infrequent rain of the desert of Sinai soaks into the thirsty plains that lie at the foot of the mountain of the Law.

SOME NOTES ON THE TRANSLATION

OF

The English Bible

INTO

THE ANCIENT BRITISH TONGUE.

*[The dates of the editions of the Welsh Bibles—subsequent
to those of Bishops Morgan, Parry and Lloyd—are
principally taken from Mr. Dore's " Old Bibles"
referred to previously.]*

SOME NOTES ON THE TRANSLATION OF THE BIBLE INTO WELSH.

So little is generally known of the history of the
translation of the Bible into the British tongue, that a
brief outline of its course may be of interest, especially to
Welshmen.

As in the case of the translation into English it was a
matter of gradual growth. In England fragments of the
Bible, such as the Pentateuch and the Psalter, were translated into Anglo-Saxon long before John Wycliffe, in 1383,
gave us the first, though not complete, translation of the
Bible into English—the basis of all subsequent editions
from that date down to the Revised Version of 1885.

The history of the Welsh MSS. of the Bible seems to
be uncertain and obscure. In fact, little is known of the
ancient history of Wales except what Prof. Rhys and his
colleagues read on the corners of gate-posts, or on stones
found in pig-styes.

Mr. Dore, in his book on "Old Bibles," says :—"That only one manuscript translation of any part of the Bible into Welsh has been known, and that was a Welsh version of the Pentateuch." He does not, however, say whether it be now extant, and if so, where it is, nor does he give the date.

On the other hand a Welsh clergyman asserts :—"That in 1282 there existed a Welsh copy of the four Gospels in MS. in S. Asaph Cathedral, and it was then considered a very old copy. In that year permission was given to the Cathedral Clergy by the Archbishop of Canterbury to take this copy of the Gospels about the Principality for exhibition." He also says "that this invaluable treasure was lost at the accession of Queen Elizabeth, when the Bishop of S. Asaph (Dr. Goldwell) was deposed"—but he gives us no authority for either statement.

In 1557 some fragments of the Bible were translated from the Vulgate into the Welsh language, and, to pass from legend to history, a few years later, A.D. 1562, the translation of the whole Bible into Welsh was commanded by Act of Parliament.

The Statute 5 Eliz. c. 28 enacts :—"That the Bible containing the New Testament and the Old, together with the Book of Common Prayer, should be translated into the British or Welsh tongue, and should be viewed, perused and allowed by the Bishops of S. Asaph, Bangor, S. David's, Llandaff and Hereford; and should be printed and used in the churches, by the 1st. of March in the year 1566, under a penalty, in case of failure, of forty pounds to be levied on each of the above Bishops."

"That one printed copy, at least, of the translation should be had for every cathedral and church, &c., throughout Wales, to be read by the Clergy in time of Divine Service, and at other times, for the benefit and perusal of any who had a mind to go to Church for that purpose : as the inhabitants of Wales (being no small part of the realm) are utterly destituted of God's Holy Word, and do remain in the like or even more darkness, than they were in the tymes of Papistry."

" And ever after, English Bibles and Common Prayers should be had and remain in every church, &c., throughout the country, with the Welsh translation, so that such as do not understand the English language, may by conferring both tongues together, the sooner attain to a knowledge of the English tongue, anything in this Act to the contrary notwithstanding."

It may not be amiss to remember here that about this period Wales was being gradually welded on to the Kingdom of England. As early as the reign of Edward I, the ancient line of the Princes of Wales was abolished, the country conquered, and the eldest son of the King of England proclaimed Prince of Wales at Carnarvon Castle. The *Statutum Walliæ* (The Statute of Wales) dated from Rhuddlan in Flintshire, enacts :—That the territory of Wales was then annexed to the dominions of the Crown of England. It runs :—" Terra Walliæ, cum incolis suis, prius nobis jure feodali subjecta, jam in proprietatis nostræ dominium totaliter et cum integrite conversa est, et coronæ regni Angliæ, tanquam pars corporis ejusdem annexa et unita."

In English :—

" The Land of Wales, with its inhabitants, formerly subjected to us by feudal right, has now been brought entirely into the rule of our own Kingdom, and united to the Crown of England, as a part of the same body."

But it was not till A.D. 1536, a few years before the

first authorised translation of the Bible into Welsh, that the laws of the two countries were assimilated.

By 27 Hen. VIII it was enacted :—

I.—That the dominion of Wales shall be for ever united to the Kingdom of England.

II.—That all Welshmen born shall have the same liberties as other the King's subjects.

III.—That lands in Wales shall be inheritable according to the English tenure.

IV.—That the laws of England and no others shall be used in Wales.

By a later Statute of the same reign (34 and 35 Hen. VIII, 26) the Principality was divided into Shires, in analogy to the territorial divisions of England. Although the English Law ran in Wales from the time of Hen. VIII, it was administered by Welsh Judges, who were independent of Westminster Hall, and it was not until the reign of William IV, that by Statute 1 W. IV, cap. 70, the Welsh Courts were finally abolished, and the administration of Justice made uniform with that of England.

This uniformity of law in the two countries, enacted in the reign of the Eighth Henry, existed until the passing of the "WELSH SUNDAY CLOSING ACT" a few years ago. Heu mihi!!

One year after the time appointed by the Statute of the 5th. Eliz., to wit in 1567, the first New Testament ever printed in Welsh, was issued. "It was printed" says Mr. Dore, "by Henry Denham, at the cost and charges of Humphrey Poy, in a handsome quarto volume of 399 leaves, similar to the Blank Stone Mole and Engravers' mark of Tyndale, black-letter type, not divided into verses, but with arguments and contents to each book and chapter." But he does not tell us who Henry Denham and Humphrey Poy may have been. There is in the preliminary matter a dedication *in English* to "the most vertuous and noble PRINCE (sic) Elizabeth, by the Grace of God, of England, France and Ireland, Queene, Defender of the Faith, &c." This dedication was signed by William Salesbury, Thomas Huet, *Chantor Menevensis;* and Dr. Richard Davis, *Menevensis.*

The last named, Dr. Davis, was a native of Denbigh, and was educated at Oxford. He was consecrated Bishop of St. Asaph in 1560 and translated to the see of St. David in 1561. He was one of the Bishops selected by Archbishop Parker to revise the Bible of 1568, commonly called "The Bishops' Bible" (see "Owen's *Pembrokeshire*" p. 240, note 5.)

This dedication is noteworthy, and in many ways so interesting as to merit full reproduction.

It supports—what has been held as more than a theory, that the Welsh people were never very devout servants of the great prelate and prince—whose humility assumed the title of "Servant of Servants," any more than they were loyal subjects of a priestly power whose more than mundane magnificence proclaimed ITSELF "Vice-gerent of God." It is a good example of the adulatory dedication to great persons that embellished our literature down to the time of Lord Chesterfield, and it also expounds for the admonition of the more recent "Wales for the Welsh" party, that their ancestors held the absorbtion of their country into the English Realm

A BOON TO THE LIBERTIES OF THE WELSH PEOPLE.

TEXT OF THE DEDICATION OF THE FIRST WELSH NEW
TESTAMENT TO QUEEN ELIZABETH, A.D. 1567.

" To the most vertuous, etc.,

When I call to remembrance, as well the face of the
corrupted religion in England, at what time Paules Churche-
yarde in the citie was occupied by makers of alabaster
images to be set up in churches, and they of Pater-noster-
rowe earned their lyving by making Pater-noster bedes,
they of Ave-lane by selling Ave bedes, and of Crede-lane
by making Crede bedes.

As also the vaine rites crept into our Country of Wales,
when instead of the lyving God, men worshipped dead
images of wood and stone, bells and bones, with such other
uncertain reliques I wot not what.

And withal consider our late general revolt from
Goddes most holie word once receaved, and dayly heare of
the like enforced uppon our brethren in forain countreys,
having most piteously susteined great calamaties, bitter
afflictions, and merciless persecutions, under which many
do yet still remayne.

I cannot, most Christian Prince, and gracious Soveraine,
but even as did the poore blynde Bartimeus or Samaritane
leper to our Saviour, so I come before your Majesties feet,
and there lying prostrate, not only for myself, but for the
delivery of my country folkes, from the spiritual blyndness
of ignorance, and foul infection of the old idolatrie and
false superstition, most humbly and dutifully to acknow-
ledge your incomparable benefit bestowed upon us in
graunting the sacred Scriptures (the verye remedie and salve
to our ghostlie blyndness and leprosie) to be had in our
best knowen tongue; which as far as ever I can gather
(through Christs true religion sometime flourished among
our ancestors the old Britons) yet were never so entirely

and universally had, as we now, God be thanked, have them.

Our countrymen in tymes passed were indeed most loth (and that not without good cause) to reseave the Romish religion, and yet have they now synce: such is the *domage* (injury) of evill custome: ben loth to forsake the same, and to receave the gospell of Christ.

But after that thys nation, as it is thought for their apostasy, had been sore plagued with long wars, *and finally vanquished*, and by rigorous laws kept under, yet at last it pleased God of his accustomed clemency, to look down again on them, sending a godly and noble David and a wise Solomon. I mean Henry VII., and Henry VIII.,—both Kynges of most famous memory and your graces grand-father and father, who graciously released their paynes, and mitigated their intolerable burdens, the one with Charters of Liberty—and the other with Acts of Parliament; by abandoning from them all bondage and thraldom, and

INCORPORATING THEM WITH HIS OTHER LOVING SUBJECTS OF ENGLAND.

This no doubt was no small benefit touching bodily wealth, but this benefit of Your Majesties providence and goodness exceedeth that other as the soule doeth the body.

* * * * * * * *

But to conclude and draw nere to offer up my vowe: where as I, by our most vigilant Pastours, the Bishops of Wales, am called and substituted, though unworthy, somewhat to deale in the perusing and setting fourth of this so worthy, a matter, I think it my most bounden duty here in their name (as the chiefest first fruict) to present to your majesty, a booke of the New Testament of our Lorde Jesus Christ, translated into the British language, which is our vulgare tongue.

And wishing, and most humbly praying, if it should so seem good to your wysedome, that it might remain in your M. Library, for a perpetual monument of your graciouse bounte, shewed herein to our countrey and the Church of Christ.

And would to God that your Graces subjects of Wales might also have *the whole book* of Gods word brought to like pass; then might their fellow subjects of England rejoice of them in these words:—The people who sat in darkness have seen a great Lyght, &c.

And thus to end, I beseech Almytye God that as your Grace's circumspect providence doth perfectlie accomplish and discharge your princely vocation and governaunce towards all your humble subjects, that we may also on our part towards God and your highness, demean ourselves in such wyse, that his justice abrydge not these halcyon and quiet days (which hetherto, since the beginning of your happie reigne, have most calmly and peaceably continued) but that we may long enjoy your gracious presence and most prosperous reigne over us: which we beseech God most mercifully to graunt us.

Your Majestie's
Most humble and faithful Subject,
William Salesbury.

The first known complete Bible in the Welsh language was a folio edition. It is dated A.D. 1558, and is known as

I.—Bishop Morgan's Bible, 1558.

It is said to have been translated from the original languages (?) by Dr. William Morgan, afterwards Bishop of St. Asaph. It contains the Old and New Testament and the so called Apochryphal Books. We say "so called" because the reason why the book which Bishop Coverdale of Exeter called " Salomon's Balettes," should be considered *inspired*, and "Ecclesiasticus," and the "Wisdom of Solomon" *not inspired*, is one of those conundrums, that in the words of Longfellow :—

> " In vain
> Perplex men's heart and brain."

The chapters in this Bible are divided into verses, and it has a long Latin dedication to Queen Elizabeth signed

GULIELMUS MORGANUS.

It was printed in London by Christopher Barker.

It is not very widely known that in 1575 Christopher Barker purchased a patent from Queen Elizabeth for the exclusive printing of Bibles, and from 1576 to 1618 nearly all English Bibles published were printed by Christopher or Robert Barker. Of the Genevan Version alone they published about 40 editions.

After keeping and using the patent for about 130 years, it passed early in the 18th. century into the hands of the Basketts, who published, amongst other Editions, the well-known "Vinegar Bible," which contained so many other mistakes, that it was also called "The Baskettful of Errors."

The Basketts held the patent for about 60 years, and then sold it to John Eyre, of Landford, Wilts, who was succeeded by his son. This son, Charles Eyre took into partnership John Strahan, and from them it passed into the worthy, capable, and careful hands of the present possessors :—

" George Eyre and William Spottiswoode, Printers to the Queen's most excellent Majesty."

Mr. Dore says that, as in the case of Miles Coverdale's Bible, Bishop Morgan's assistants in the translation are unknown, but it is curious that amongst those who are supposed to have contributed their help we find the name of the Rev. Richard Vaughan, Rector of the parish of Lutterworth, the living held by John Wycliffe some two hundred years before. The number of copies of this edition issued is not exactly known, but it was small, and supposed not to have exceeded one thousand.

A quarto edition of the Prayer Book and Psalter was printed in black letter during the same year, 1558.

II.—Bishop Parry's Bible, A.D. 1620.

In this year a revision of Bishop Morgan's Bible was undertaken by his successor in the see of St. Asaph, Dr. Richard Parry, and was printed in London, in folio, by Bonham Norton and John Bill.

The emendations and alterations made by Doctor Parry were so numerous and important as to make his Book more a new translation than a revision of an old one. A copy of this Bible was presented to James I and is now in the British Museum. The marginal references are taken from King James's Bible of 1611.

There is a dedication in Latin to King James, and in it Dr. Parry says:

That the copies of Morgan's Bible being exhausted and many or most of the Welsh churches being without Bibles, or having only worn or unperfect copies, he set about revising the Welsh Bible, as the English Bible had recently been revised (Authorised Version, 1611), for the sake of providing for his countrymen a better and more correct version than they had ever possessed.

This Bible is supposed to have been translated directly from the Hebrew and Greek Versions, and not merely from the English Version into Welsh, and is the Authorised

Welsh Version at present used in places of Worship in the Principality belonging to the "Church of England."

The first octavo Bible published in the Welsh language is said on the title page to have been printed in London (Printiedig yn Llundain) by Robert Barker, A.D. 1630.

The text is in Roman type. This edition was undertaken, like other Welsh and English Bibles, not by any public authority, but by private persons on their own responsibility and risk. "Sir Thos. Middleton and Mr. Rowland Heylyn, both Aldermen of London and natives of Wales, co-operating with two other gentlemen, undertook to supply the great want of a Bible of suitable size for family and private reading. The reason why the Bible in Welsh, says Mr. Dore, was so sparingly supplied was to induce the Welsh people to study the English language for the purpose of obtaining a knowledge of the Scriptures, and thus gradually to banish the ancient British tongue from the Principality and to substitute for it the English language.

III.—Bishop Lloyd's Bible, A.D. 1690.

The third folio edition of the Bible in Welsh was published in 1690, and is known as "Lloyd's Bible." It was printed at the Theatre, Oxford, in Roman letters, and was brought out under the superintendence of Mr. Pierce Lewis, an Anglesea man, of Jesus College, Oxford. It does not profess to be a new translation, but merely a faithful reprint of Bishop Parry's Bible of 1620.

IV. The octavo edition of the Welsh Bible of 1654, consisting of 6000 copies, soon became exhausted, and in 1677 another octavo issue was produced of 8000 copies. One thousand were distributed gratuitously amongst the poor, and the remainder were offered for sale at four shillings each—(Dore).

V. In 1667, an octavo edition was published under the care of Mr. Stephen Hughes, of Swansea, and freely circulated through private benevolence.

VI. In 1689 a quarto edition of the Welsh Bible was printed by Bill and Newcombe, London, in small and poor type. A considerable portion of the expense of the issue was defrayed by the Earl of Warton, once a member of Queen Anne's Cabinet, and ten thousand copies were issued.

18TH. CENTURY WELSH BIBLES.

VII. In 1718, an octavo edition printed in London, edited by the Rev. Moses Williams, Vicar of Dyfynog, Brecon, and published, as were the two following editions, by the Society for Promoting Christian Knowledge.

VIII. The second edition, in octavo, of the eighteenth Century, was published in 1727 without contents of chapters, or marginal references, and for this reason was very little valued by the Welsh people.

IX. In 1746, another octavo edition was printed by J. Bentham, Caer Grawnt, "and had besides the Old and New Testament, the Apochrypha, the Prayer Book, and a Metrical Psalter by Archdeacon Pryse."

X. In 1752, under the care of Mr. Morris Baskett (the publisher of the Bible of 1719, sometimes called the Vinegar Bible, and sometimes, on account of its many mistakes, the Baskettful of Errors) was published another octavo edition. This particular "Basket," however, was considered the most correct Welsh Bible ever published.

XI.—A quarto edition was printed at Carmarthen in 1770, with a Welsh concordance, and also two octavos, one in the same year and the other in 1799.

82

It has been mentioned before that two of the translators of the first Welsh New Testament, were Richard Davies,
Bishop, and Thomas Huet, Precentor, of St. David's.

In "The description of Pembrokeshire," written by
the Lord of Kemes in the sixteenth century, the 25th.
chapter treats "Of diverse famouse and learned men, that
hath lived and been borne in the county of Penbrok in
former tyme, whose works are left and be extante to the
posteritie."

After mention of S. Patrick and Merlin, George Owen
refers to these two worthies of the chapter of S. David's as
follows :

"Richard Davides, Bushopp of S. Davides, a man noe
lesse in his tyme much reverenced for his rare vertues, and
excellencie in learneing, agreeable to his place and calling,
than honoured for his publique hospitallitie, and liberalitie
in his liffe-tyme. Though sustaineinge menye trobles and
greate crosses, yett soe bearing himself, as he was inwardly
affected of the good, and never detracted but of the bad;
he for the advancement of God's glorie translated into
Welsh :—1. The Newe Testament. 2. The Common Praier
Book. 3. Many notable sermons. He died 7 November,
1581."

"Thomas Huet, Chaunter of S. David's, a man that all
his liffe bare himself able waies in good accompt and
estimacion, took alsoe much paines with the said Bushopp
Davides, in translateing the former books as may appear
by the epistles of them He died on 19th August, 1591."

The foregoing is a brief and imperfect outline of the
history of the Welsh Bible, from its translation down to the
commencement of the nineteenth century.

THE END.

CPSIA information can be obtained at www.ICGtesting.com
Printed in the USA
BVOW01s1057141014

370745BV00020B/555/P

9 781271 679683